THE POWER OF THE HOUR

Annunya Sankhua

Chennai • Bangalore

CLEVER FOX PUBLISHING
Chennai, India

Published by CLEVER FOX PUBLISHING 2024
Copyright © Annunya Sankhua 2024

All Rights Reserved.
ISBN: 978-93-56488-19-9

This book has been published with all reasonable efforts taken to make the material error-free after the consent of the author. No part of this book shall be used, reproduced in any manner whatsoever without written permission from the author, except in the case of brief quotations embodied in critical articles and reviews.

The Author of this book is solely responsible and liable for its content including but not limited to the views, representations, descriptions, statements, information, opinions and references ["Content"]. The Content of this book shall not constitute or be construed or deemed to reflect the opinion or expression of the Publisher or Editor. Neither the Publisher nor Editor endorse or approve the Content of this book or guarantee the reliability, accuracy or completeness of the Content published herein and do not make any representations or warranties of any kind, express or implied, including but not limited to the implied warranties of merchantability, fitness for a particular purpose. The Publisher and Editor shall not be liable whatsoever for any errors, omissions, whether such errors or omissions result from negligence, accident, or any other cause or claims for loss or damages of any kind, including without limitation, indirect or consequential loss or damage arising out of use, inability to use, or about the reliability, accuracy or sufficiency of the information contained in this book.

Dedication

This book is dedicated to my two most important people: my husband, Mr Adithya Manimaran, who has always taught me to be humble, receive feedback gracefully, and keep doing my best.

My son, Master Vivaan Adithya, who has always taught me to be happy without any reason and never give up.

Contents

About the Author v
Introduction vii
Prologue ix

  1. Acknowledge That You're Not Proficient At Managing Your Time 1
  2. The Power of One 3
  3. Assign Deadlines to Each Task 5
  4. Write Down Your Goals 9
  5. Avoid Distractions 13
  6. Be Sure to Reward Yourself 17
  7. Art of Delegation 19
  8. Art of Saying NO 21
  9. Say No to Multitasking 25
  10. Schedule Everything 31
  11. Value Your Time 35

Summary 39
A Story To Share 41
Epilogue 45
Acknowledgments 47

About the Author

*A*nnunya Sankhua is a human behavior analyst, parent coach, public speaker, and image consultant. Her dominant area in training includes Nonverbal (which essentially is body language and voice variety) & Verbal communication, and Emotional Intelligence.

She assists people in creating a lasting first impression and understanding the art of clustering and styling outfits.

With a MBA in Systems and HR, she comes with a working experience of over 7+ years with various industries like retail, hospitality, and IT. Her last assignment was with RBS as a Business Support Analyst. She was also associated with the Lifeline Foundation as a volunteer.

Two things that made her venture into the training industry:

1. With all these industries, 'be it be the front end or the back end'; there was one constant element, 'THE PEOPLE,' which fascinated her to venture into the industry of training that is ALL ABOUT PEOPLE.
2. Since childhood, she has been curious, inquisitive, and interested to know more, know why, and know-how? And this curiosity led her to be a trainer, to understand what makes people tick? WHY DO THEY DO WHAT THEY DO?

Annunya is a highly empathetic and skilled communicator who connects with people effortlessly. Traveling, writing blogs and quotes, sketching, coloring, dancing, kickboxing, and wardrobe styling are some of her favorite activities. She is a wife, mother to a cute son, and an ardent animal lover.

Introduction

"You will never 'find' time for anything. If you want time, you must make it."
— **Charles Buxton**

"Productivity is never an accident. It is always the result of a commitment to excellence, intelligent planning, and focused effort."
— **Paul J Meyer**

"Either Run the day
   or
The day runs you."

— **Jim Rohn**

We all live in an illusion that we have a lot of time, time for everything. However, the reality is different; time is non-refundable, non-negotiable, and non-stoppable.

Make the best use of the time so that tomorrow we can sit and say, "I did, spend it wisely."

Prologue

*D*ang! Ugh, the alarm rings and irritates Riya; she gets up and thinks to herself, "Why the hell do I sleep late, and why the hell do I wake up late?". She gets her bed tea and is too lazy to move herself! The day begins with the phone, that mini virtual world which one misses as they sleep and grabs at once as they are awake. Her eyes wander across her mobile as she sips her tea, and one thing leads to another and another, and she has no idea why she has been on the phone for so many hours.

And, when she sees the clock, it's already 9:30 am, and she has to rush to do her job. Somehow, she gets ready and continues her task of the day, juggling, cribbing, and cursing herself that she is so terrible at managing her time. But the most disappointing part is that she still gets distracted by the mini device, despite knowing that it's a distraction.

Truth be told, I have been there. It appeared as though my time was on the run because I was not managing time; instead, it made me restless, inattentive, and angry. So, what did I do to take charge of the time? About which I knew I could not hold or stop?

What Power do I have to take Control of my hour?

I am sure you must have a lot of ideas on your mind, like a timetable, calendar, etc. However, I didn't do anything about the timetable or calendar to start with. You cannot expect a baby to run on day one, can you?

As ineffective as I have been with my time management skill,

I have listed the methods I use and have been using to manage my time in the following chapters.

CHAPTER 1

ACKNOWLEDGE THAT YOU'RE NOT PROFICIENT AT MANAGING YOUR TIME

*M*ilk overflowed and spilled, the gas stove messed with last night's cooking, and the kitchen sink filled with unwashed utensils. Riya, in her yellow t-shirt and blue pajamas with messy hair standing in the kitchen, her mind filled with all the things she needs to get done. Still, she is unable to decide where to begin with. As she grumbled to herself, she was doing everything possible to finish all the work, but it was not enough. She wished there were 48 hours in a day instead of 24 hours. She always believed that she had more work and less time and was doing her finest to manage everything. She was efficient and knew what she had to do. She was in constant denial that the work was more, not the time that had to be appropriately managed.

I've been there, and I have been in constant denial about my time management skills.

The acceptance of the fact that I am inadequate to manage my time was the toughest. I was in denial with excuses that my hands were full, and I was doing what I could. But the reoccurring event of not having enough time every day made me realize that I am awful at time management and have to work on it. The first step to improvement begins when we acknowledge our shortcomings. So, I took the first baby step to accept my inadequacy.

Because time is one thing which remains the same for everyone, rich or poor, kid or adult, working or nonworking, and once it's gone, it's gone as Geoffrey Chaucer aptly stated, **"TIME AND TIDE WAIT FOR NONE."**

CHAPTER 2

THE POWER OF ONE

During those days, there was no Netflix, Amazon Prime, or Hotstar, so our mothers had to wait for television serials to air at a specific time. Before the TV serial started, they used to finish all their household chores, make their dinner, and make sure the children finished their homework so that they could watch the serial peacefully. The telecast time was fixed, and to abide by the time of the serial, they completed everything before the serial time; and voila, they knowingly or unknowingly managed their time by keeping one particular event constant.

Therefore, by setting that one task for a day, you are trying to get the other tasks done before your fixed task.

For people like me who don't know how to manage their time, this is a simple tip: start with one thing, the simplest and easiest task you know you have to complete every day and keep it up for 21 days till it's embedded in your subconscious mind. For me, my exercise was a priority to do it daily, and so I decided to pick a time and stick to it.

And to stick to a particular time, I had to finish all the other tasks before it, so that was the baby step to getting things done.

You might have something that you love; it may be reading a book, watching tv, cooking, etc. Do schedule that one thing.

This step personally has helped me to an extent in getting my time management skills on point. I call it **"THE POWER OF ONE,"** remember, one is better than none. Start with that one thing; other things will fall into place eventually.

CHAPTER 3

ASSIGN DEADLINES TO EACH TASK

I bet everyone remembers their exam days. I prepared for my 10th board exam within 18 days I spent studying. Now I never scored 80%, and that's not what we are talking about, but I completed my preparation in 18 days, which means a whole year wasn't sufficient, but 18 days made a difference. Huh! Strange!!

Remember how you had one month to submit your project, and you got it done only in the eleventh hour. Well, if you happen to be among the 2 percent who finish the job in the first week, kudos to you, but I fall in the remaining

98% who wait till the last week or maybe the previous day to finish the project.

So set a deadline for any project, stick to it strictly, and you will see the results.

According to Parkinson's law, work expands in order to fill the time available for its completion. Therefore, the more time you commit to a task, the longer it will take you to accomplish it. Because our brain says, "ABHI TOH TIME HAI" (there is still time)

Take this book, for that matter, this is my first book, and I have been trying to write for a long time, for like 4 to 5 years; however, this book was completed in 7 days. Yes, you read it correctly in 7 days. All drafting and redrafting, creating and re-creating, and everything.

This is what happens when you set a time limit.

Fun fact, your creativity increases when you know that you have a time crunch, and you have to think and come out of your comfort zone. Try it, you will know it; it has happened with me every single damn time. At the last moment, I will have an "EUREKA MOMENT."

CHAPTER 4

WRITE DOWN YOUR GOALS

*U*ntil the day before her birthday, I remembered to wish her. However, on the day of her birthday, I completely forgot to do so. When I remembered after two days, the damage had already been done, so it took me a while to make up for the blunder.

I take pride in keeping everything in my mind, be it be birthdays, names, and to-do lists. As good as my memory power is, but it has ditched me when needed the most. My husband always tells me, "Why cannot you write down your things and keep them? If you cannot write, at least keep a reminder on the phone."

There is no doubt about the fact that we all have super brainpower, but we tend to forget things and only remember when we see them. It is the "POWER OF VISUALIZATION."

Tell me, how many times has Facebook reminded you of a birthday that you forgot? I bet, a lot many times.

I realized rather than keeping reminders, which, of course, is a good idea, I preferred writing my goals along with the deadlines cause goals without the set time are going to be a never-ending affair.

And you must be wondering why writing?

Because

i) You feel more relaxed when you write things down, and it helps reduce stress.
ii) You feel more in control of your life when you write things down.
iii) When you write down your goals, they become more noteworthy; you hold on to them.

iv) You feel accomplished and progress as you cross items off your to-do list. Doing this motivates you to keep going when things get tough.

So, I started separating my short-term goals and long-term goals along with deadlines to meet my goals, and I put it on the wall at my eye level, and when I complete my task, I keep ticking it off the chart. I cannot tell you the happiness of completing the task on hand. I am sure it must be a joy for you too when you complete a project or job.

Alternatively, if you are like my husband, who doesn't like writing, I would suggest keeping reminders on your phones, yes, the mini electronic diary let's put it to productive use because something is better than nothing.

Though I am a pen and paper person, I do use the mini electronic diary to keep reminding me to drink water.

CHAPTER 5

AVOID DISTRACTIONS

$\mathcal{H}$ow do I focus when my environment is full of distractions? Asked Riya, whose attention span is minimal, she is disappointed, frustrated, and annoyed. She knows that she is distracted and cannot bring it under her control.

I can very well relate to her agony. I remember my mom while cooking, getting bugged whenever there used to be a doorbell; I never understood why? I used to think, "what's so big a deal about the doorbell?"

Now, when I think I can connect the dots. Whenever the doorbell rang while my mother was in the kitchen trying to complete the cooking, she had to rush to attend to it.

And she came back, every time either she got absorbed in something else, and the cooking got delayed, or she would take more time to finish the cooking as she had to recollect the whole process where she was during the cooking.

Do you know that it takes approximately 30 minutes to refocus after being distracted? According to University of California Irvine study, "it takes an average of 23 minutes and 15 seconds to get back to the task." So, every time you get distracted, be sure that you will need more time to do what you were doing.

Yes, I agree, to get distracted is normal and happens, but we can control it. YES, we can!

Now, how?

There is a technique called the Pomodoro technique, and it consists of 5 simple steps,

i) Select the task that you need to work on.
ii) Set the timer to 25 mins (use an alarm clock or phone timer will do, there are apps too)

iii) Work on the task till the timer rings (no cheating here)
iv) Take a five mins break (put an alarm for that too)
v) After four cycles of the same, take a 15 to 30 min break.

I use the Pomodoro technique for myself as well as for my 6-year-old son to make him study. I know you are surprised, and let me tell you, he enjoys the process of learning. I keep 20 mins of study time with 10 mins break time. I keep a timer for both of them, this continues for four cycles which are 80 mins study and 40 mins of break, and after four cycles of the same, I give him an interval of 1 hour, if pending studies are there, we again repeat the process otherwise we stop it. And there's more focus during studies and fewer distractions as it's clear that he will be getting a break every 20 mins.

Now coming to the mini world that is your mobile, and if it's your distraction, then you can

a) Put off the Wi-Fi or mobile data so that the continuous beep sound doesn't tempt you to go back.
b) Switch off the notifications.
c) Delete the apps that distract you. Why? Because it will be a long process to install again and log in.

Now, I have no solution to your doorbell; maybe a DND (do not disturb) sign will help!

CHAPTER 6

BE SURE TO REWARD YOURSELF

I was fascinated by literature, and I used to put my heart and soul in writing. And when my teacher used to praise me and give an A+, I would always be looking forward to performing better and more efficiently. And it's an obvious fact that everyone likes to be rewarded, don't we? So, why wait for anyone to pat your back, reward yourself by patting your back, and self-incentivize.

My way of self-incentivizing is giving myself a break time to watch television for 30 mins or pampering myself with a massage or just sleeping, or doing anything which makes me feel relaxed, happy, and rejuvenated.

The Power of the Hour

To each its own, whatever works for you, go ahead and do reward and pamper yourself. In short, make yourself feel good for doing a good job.

This way, you will take a pause, compose, and get recharged for your next step.

And the reward becomes sweeter when you know it comes after hard work.

CHAPTER 7

ART OF DELEGATION

Pihu was running late for attending her training session, but she was juggling and struggling to complete her household chores. It was admirable that she did all her job by herself. And She does take pride in flaunting so! However, managing everything at home, work, and studies often drained her of her energy, making her cry, crib, and yell at herself and others. What do you think could be the reason for her sorry plight? It's evident that she takes all the responsibilities and balancing them becomes problematic at times.

Have you been like her? Because I sure have been, and it has left me shattered. And I found out the secret, that is to delegate the work to someone who can fill in your shoes. I understand,

and I agree we all have our way to do things, and maybe we don't like others to interfere and do it their way (if you are like me). Well, we can always tell and teach them to do things in the way we want to.

Pihu sure did get domestic help to help her with household chores, and guess what, now she was happy and more focused on her work and studies.

Yes, I too have let go of the habit of doing everything by myself. And I agree it was a bit difficult; however, I have the time to focus on what's more important for me.

Let go of the small jobs that can be taught and delegated to others. We cannot be everywhere every time. Even God delegates because he cannot be everywhere; that's why he created Mother!!

CHAPTER 8

ART OF SAYING NO

*A*fter dropping my son off at school, I stood near my Activa and shuffled my handbag. I was looking for my phone and the bike key when I heard someone calling, "Hey, Annunya, how have you been??" I turned around to see my friend Sheena in her usual corporate attire, white shirt, black pant, and black blazer standing a few feet away from me. It was a delight to meet her, and we chatted for some time, and then she told me to join her in some webinar regarding an MLM (Multi-level Marketing) business.

And all my to-do lists were popping in my mind and asking me to tell a "NO." But as a YES person, I blurted a "Yes" reluctantly. Yeah! yeah, I am a people pleaser, and I have difficulty in saying

"NO." And yeah, I wasted my precious two hours attending the webinar with her. After that, she again called me to join the next level, but this time I gathered all my courage and politely told her, "Thank you, Sheena, for the invite, but I am sorry, this isn't my cup of tea." She understood that I was not interested.

I cannot express in words what a sense of achievement it was, just saying a NO. For me, declining and saying NO was a battle, and I was the winner by just telling the two letters, "N" and "O."

How many of you have wasted your precious hours just because you cannot say a simple 'No'? As you can see, I have a lot of times, prioritizing my job was a difficult task.

Most of us find it difficult to say "NO" even though we know that we are going to spend our time just like that, and needless to say, we are people pleasers because "LOG BURA MANJAYENGE" (people will feel bad) is more important to us than our priorities.

I learned the hard way to say "No"; let me make that simple for you,

i) Be assertive and not arrogant. You can always thank them for the invite, or the proposal and tell them sorry that you cannot accept it. And when you thank for the invite or proposal, do mean it and be genuine about it.
ii) Don't reason it out because the other side will always try to offer a solution. You know your priorities better.
iii) Try to provide an alternative, which means you are ready to do something else together if not the present thing. For instance, if you cannot make it to the dinner party, offer them if they want a quick catch-up over a coffee.

When you learn to say **"No"** to non-important stuff, you learn to say **"Yes"** to all the important stuff.

CHAPTER 9

SAY NO TO MULTITASKING

*I*n the middle of the night, Riya got up with a jerk. She looked around; AC was on at 22, the fan was on at 5, and the thin pullover was on her. But she was sweating and panting as though she had seen a ghost. She sat on her bed and couldn't understand what was happening. So, she came out of the bed, went to the hall, and sat on the two-seater blue sofa; a pile of pending work that had to be completed was running through her mind.

She happens to be a voracious reader, and her bookshelf is full of books. However, only a few of them read while others were still sitting on the shelf waiting for her to be opened. She isn't into the television much, but she has her favorite series marked, which are still un-played or half played.

Sitting there, lost in her thoughts, she was totally blank. She wanted to do so many things.

She wants to take care of her social media account, watch tv-series and movies, read books, complete her courses, travel, and many more. But here she was sitting and trying to do everything in one shot.

Reading about Riya, how many of you thought, this is so ME! I sure thought I wanted to tick mark everything at one go because "KAL HO NA HO" (who has seen tomorrow), and if you are not like her, congratulations, I would definitely love to meet you.

Multitasking is nothing, but it's like an urge to eat everything on your plate at one time, practically is it possible? In my opinion, not at all.

As I said, I was like Riya; the constant thought that I had to do this and do that was frustrating. I suffered from insomnia, rolling over in the bed, changing sides, and trying to sleep. Neither my days nor my nights were peaceful. In the long run, it just made me angry.

I have met multitaskers who take pride in exhibiting that they can focus on more than one task at a time. But can you really? Technically you cannot because our brain can focus only on one thing at a time. One cannot jump the whole stairs together; S/he has to go one step at a time.

You can argue that there are situations where you have to multitask. I agree there are, and there will be, but when we multitask, we tend to miss out on something or the other, and as a result, we have to refocus and rework.

Thanks to the advent of technologies, I love shopping online now that almost everything is available online. However, you feel like going out and shopping for groceries or apparel or maybe stationaries once in a while. So it happened, my son and I went for a walk to a faraway garden, and by that garden was a vast nursery. I have a strong love for plants, specifically indoor ones. I saw a bamboo plant, and I wanted to get it for my home. As I looked and selected the plant I would like to buy, and my phone started ringing. While I was answering the call, I showed the shopkeeper the plant I would like to take and kept an eye on my son, who was busy observing the plants. It was 520 rupees, and I took out my wallet and paid him the amount. On my way back in the auto, while I was speaking to my son, suddenly a thought crossed my mind, "Did I pay the shopkeeper a 500 rupees note or a 2000 rupees note?" I checked my wallet and tried to recall the notes I had; I counted and recounted what I feared came true. I had given the shopkeeper 2000 rupees instead of 500.

How many of you think that, had I not answered the call, I would have saved 1500 rupees? I sure do and regret.

Shopping, talking over the phone, and looking after a child - doing all three together was a terrible idea.

If you remember, when we are on a call and if someone asks us anything, we generally tend to say "yes" without even properly understanding or realizing what we are saying yes to. That's the blunder of multitasking.

Multitasking may make you feel like you are doing a lot of work, but in reality, it's just a mirage, taking you nowhere and delaying your process further.

CHAPTER 10

SCHEDULE EVERYTHING

*I*t was a Friday the 12th, around 11:15 pm, and I was watching a scary horror movie, and it was about to get over. During which I had a strong urge to munch something. I got up and went to the fridge to see if there were any items to munch on, and there was nothing, so I returned and continued my movie. After precisely 10 mins, I repeated the process of getting up to the fridge to encounter the same; this continued for a while till the movie was over.

Let me confess; I am obsessed with checking my phone. Social media makes me restless. The number of likes makes me check my phone and laptop frequently even though I am well aware of what will be there, like the empty fridge.

I have the habit of responding instantly whenever someone calls, emails, texts, or pings me. And because of that, I get distracted.

As already discussed in Chapter 5, avoid distractions and steps on how to do it. But what about calls in between work, what about the mails, pings which need to be answered.

Well, we can always schedule the time for the calls/ callbacks, answering the pings, messages, and emails.

Set an automated message when you disconnect the call stating them you will call them back as soon as you are available.

Select a time of the day where you can sit and reply to pings, messages, and emails.

In any case, if your attention is required and it's urgent, the caller will call you again or message you immediately. And if it's not, they can wait for your call or reply.

Schedule Everything

Also, to add on, prioritize your work and put it in your calendar, and if it's not completed, carry it forward to the next day.

In the quest to complete your work, don't forget to call your loved ones, schedule calls with them, and block the slot for the same in your calendar if you are forgetful like me.

CHAPTER 11

VALUE YOUR TIME

*I*t was the year 2020 Sunday, 7:09 pm, and I was all decked up, prepared, and ready for my online session over Zoom. It was an hour complementary session on First Impression, and already 15 people had enrolled for the same. I created the WhatsApp group for my participants and shared the meeting details, and on the day of the session, I sent them a prior reminder in the morning, afternoon, and one hour before the session to join on time. Session time was 7 pm, and me being the trainer, opened the Zoom room by 6:50 pm so that people should start joining in. And by 7:07 pm, only three people had joined. Here I was trying to manage them and asking them to wait for others to join, and by 7:17 pm, four more joined. Half-heartedly, I started my session, and by 7:35 pm, a few more joined in. The session was planned for an hour, from 7 pm to 8 pm, but it continued till 9:00 pm. I don't know if you observed, I wasted one hour because I was waiting for the participants.

This habit of mine continued for many more sessions until one day when my husband told me, "If you are supposed to start your session by a particular time, do start after waiting maybe for a maximum of 5 mins. If you respect your time, the participants will respect it." This line hit me hard; I realized it's me who isn't respecting my time.

Lesson learned - if you have scheduled a call, meeting, or a get-together and a few of your participants or guest have already joined, start the event or the session even if not everyone had joined by then. People who don't participate on time irrespective of constant reminders are the ones who are never going to make it on time, and in the long run, it is them who will miss something.

Value your time so that others will start valuing it.

Summary

*L*et's summarize the eleventh-step process for being better at time management.

1) Acceptance of your inadequacy about time management, improvements begin with acceptance.
2) Starting with one thing and getting in sequence. And it can be anything which you know is essential and must be done.
3) Allocating a timeline for each work and sticking to it. The journey is never-ending without a goal, so set a time for the task.
4) Penning your goals down and keeping them at eye level. If you are a mobile person and it's convenient for you, start with it, use Siri or Alexa to keep reminders.

5) Keep your distractions at bay, and focus. Use the Pomodoro technique to focus, and don't forget to keep your electronic devices offline.
6) Remember to pat your own back, celebrate the achievements and charge up for the next.
7) Delegate the small jobs to someone who can fill in your shoes. This way, you focus on what's important to you
8) Say NO to events and things that steal your time and help you go nowhere.
9) Multitasking creates an illusion that you are doing so many works at a time, but in reality, you can focus on one thing at a time.
10) Schedule everything, be it be a phone call with your loved ones or managing your social media accounts.
11) Value and respect your time. The moment you start sending the signal, people too will start valuing your time. It all begins with you.

A Story To Share

Five more minutes..

It was June 16, 2019, the pre-covid era. Needless to say, this is the post covid era going on. Anyway, I remember having a doctor's appointment at 3 pm. My son was in school, and from there, he would be going to the daycare, so I had time till 6:00 pm, good enough time to finish my doctor's thing and pick him up on the way. Truth be told, I was a late Latif, busy doing nothing and peaking at my watch every 5 mins and giving a buffer of 5 mins more; yep, the 5 mins more excuse.

So I got ready by 2:25 pm to start for the 3 pm appointment; watching TV and shuffling my phone made me ready by 2:25 pm. Technically, I should have started by 2:20, but me being me,

I began by 2:30, as Uber took time to arrive. For some reason, there was a bit more traffic than usual; we all know traffic, which behaves like weather, and it delayed my arrival time for the appointment, and I reached by 3:15 pm. Somehow, there were patients already in there, resulting in losing my spot and missing the appointment as the Doc had to leave for an official meeting.

With a heavy heart, almost teary eyes, and long thoughts about the missed opportunity and again rescheduling everything, I started in an Uber to pick up my son on the way back home.

And somehow I arrived 10 mins late, my son waiting alone with the teacher looking for me. Even though I apologized, the guilt was overwhelming. If I had not spent those 5 minutes watching that TV, I might have been there on time, not missed the appointment, might not have been upset, and would have arrived on time to pick my son up.

Just those 5 mins would have made an enormous difference.

The below write-up is by an unknown author, but whoever has written it s/he penned it most beautifully.

To realize the value of one year,

ask a student who failed a grade.

To realize the value of one month,

ask a mother who gave birth to a premature baby.

To realize the value of one week,

ask the editor of a weekly newspaper.

To realize the value of one day,

ask a daily wager labourer with kids to feed.

To realize the value of one hour,

ask the lovers who are waiting to meet.

To realize the value of one minute,

ask the person who missed the train.

The Power of the Hour

To realize the value of one second,

ask a person who just avoided an accident.

To realize the value of one millisecond,

ask the person who won a silver medal in the Olympics.

Epilogue

*W*e have all heard time is money, but the difference I believe between money and time is that money, if kept in a bank, can multiply, but the beauty of time is that we cannot keep it.

It's on a flow, cannot be owned, cannot be held, and cannot be kept. It has to be spent in a way you want to.

In a day, we have 1440 minutes. Invest in a way that brings you a sense of accomplishment, fulfillment, and achievement.

I have already mentioned that I have learned the hard way to spend my time wisely. My idea here is to help you be better with your time.

I live by a simple rule, "I don't need to manage time, I need to manage myself, and the time will be managed by itself.

Acknowledgments

*F*irst and foremost, I thank almighty and the universe for blessing me with the people in my life who push me to do better.

Secondly, to my parents, my Mother (Ma), Mrs Ratna Rani Sankhua, and my father (Baba), Mr Brindaban Sankhua. Whatever I am today is because of them. Their constant love, support and encouragement have always made me go one step further. I owe my risk-taking ability and becoming an independent person to them.

My second set of parents, my Mother-in-law (Amma), Mrs Kannagi Manimaran, and my father-in-law (Dad), Dr Manimaran Mari, for their never-ending appreciation, motivation, and unconditional love.

My heartfelt thanks to my husband, Mr Adithya Manimaran, for handling my mood swings and being patient with me. I know I can be a big annoying person while doing my work.

My six-year-old son Master Vivaan Adithya inspires me day in and day out. He helps me keep calm, understands me, and always tells me to go to my happy place whenever I am anxious. I don't know what I would have done without him. He makes my world beautiful and, at times, crazy.

To my brilliant nephew, Master Aarnav Sriram, who happens to be my biggest cheerleader and my best bud.

I am grateful to my younger brother Mr. Pyas Sankhua (Piu) for having my back always.

Lots of love to both my beautiful sisters-in-law Aarthi di - Mrs Aarthi Sriram and Payal - Ms Payal Panda

My sincere thanks to Mr Atanu Debnath and Mrs Amrita Debnath for being there as

Acknowledgments

guardian angels and for helping me to improve my English.

I am speechless when it comes to thanking my friends Amit, Mr Amit Nandan, Charu, Ms Charu Yadav, and Prerna, Ms Prerna Das, who always pushes me to go ahead and do it anyway.

My heartfelt thanks to Mr Jatin Gupta, popularly known as Inspiring Jatin, for helping and guiding me to publish my book.

Thirdly, thanks to all my readers for choosing this book. Remember to write to me about how this book helped you. Please do leave your feedback on Amazon. It will motivate them to read and improve their time management.

www.ingramcontent.com/pod-product-compliance
Lightning Source LLC
LaVergne TN
LVHW041553070526
838199LV00046B/1941